HUMBLINGS OF AN EVERYDAY MAN

REINHARDT BRUCKER

ATHENA PRESS
LONDON

HUMBLINGS OF AN EVERYDAY MAN
Copyright © Reinhardt Brucker 2004

ISBN 1 932077 14 6

First Published 2004 by
ATHENA PRESS
Queen's House, 2 Holly Road
Twickenham TW1 4EG
United Kingdom

Printed for Athena Press

HUMBLINGS OF AN
EVERYDAY MAN

This book is dedicated to my children who give me awareness and inspiration… Chris, Nick, Ally, Kate and Phillip… and to my darling wife, Dawn, the love of my life, my best friend, who makes life a joy and who helps create Heaven on earth for me and our family. I love you, honey.

Acknowledgements

As with so many acknowledgements, invariably there is the risk that I will forget someone. And even though I might forget the person or the face, rest assured that I will NEVER forget what you've done for me.

First of all to my parents and God, for giving me life and love.

To all the teachers throughout my life, without whom our society would crumble, I owe a debt I can never repay, but to pass on your teachings. A special thank you to Betty Saunders.

To the many friends over the 'as many' years, I say thank you for being there for me, however briefly. You have had a profound effect on who I have become. Every little nuance, good time and tragedy was worth it because you were there.

To those of you I disappointed, please forgive me. I'm still learning.

To those acquaintances who I might have met only in passing, you might have only given me a smile or a kind word, but you never knew for that moment, you probably made my day.

And to my family and extended family, you are part of me and I you. That will go on forever.

And to you the reader, I thank you for reading my words. There is nothing more humbling to have another honor me with interest in what I have to say, even though I am but one voice.

And lastly, I would remind us all to LOVE one another…

…because nothing is stronger than love.

Reinhardt Brucker

Contents

A Passion for Life

There are events in our life that form us, shape us into the person we are to become. There are more on a daily basis than we think. These are happening to us, but as well, happening to—or with someone else at the same moment. And when old memories are recalled, they are many times embellished with the years. Yet they are still significant for their value.

Such was an incident in my ninth grade gym class. We were playing "touch" football. (There's no such thing as just touch football in ninth grade) No safety equipment. I, not a true "jock type" still held my own with the guys who played every day of their lives since they were four. I was on the front line and because of Peter, who was twice my size kept being in my way, I could never get past him to get to sack the quarterback. Time after time, play after play, Peter would just stand there in his hugeness and block me, bump me or knock me over. It's not that he was an exceptional player, he was just BIG. It was like going around a huge tree's trunk and getting caught in the low hanging branches as you went by. And after getting caught, the play was over. This went on for most of the class.

In my frustration I thought, "Well, what are you gonna do? Are you just gonna wimp out and take it? Or for once are you gonna find a way past him?"

Fatigued as I was, my adrenaline kicked in.

There are times in life that make your resolve so strong that you finally want to do something about being stuck in a situation even though there's a looming obstacle in front of you. Peter was that obstacle that day. We face obstacles every day, just like "Peter". It may be we're stuck in a job or relationship we hate. We may have financial problems or physical ailments we've had for a while. And these make us very tired and worn out.

Then comes the moment where we say, "Enough! This moment I'm making a change." And as tired as we once were, just uttering those words makes us realize that we *are* still in control of ourselves, our lives, and our attitudes. We just gave control away temporarily.

I decided Peter was "going down". Even though he outweighed me by fifty plus pounds, even though I never got around him before, I thought right through the obstacle and focused on my goal of tackling the quarterback. Since the definition of "Insanity" is doing the same things you've always done and expecting a different result, I decided to do something different! I took four steps back so I could get a running start at Peter. I would hit him so hard that his Grandchildren would be born dizzy! The ball was snapped. I started to run with all my might. By the time I reached Peter, I was running at "full bore". And then… WHAMMO! Peter wasn't ready for my freight train velocity. He stumbled four or five steps backward before he finally fell out of my way flat onto the ground! The next thing I recall is having the quarterback's neck in a headlock on our way down to the ground. He never even got a chance to throw the ball. I did it! I broke through! It was not the physical breakthrough as much as it was the psychological one that was bigger.

And the satisfaction was complete when I heard the other team say on the next play, "Somebody cover Brucker over there!" I was finally considered a formidable adversary to the other team! A passion for life awakened! Passionate awakenings happen regularly throughout my life, even today.

I don't remember any other sporting successes like that one, but that one was enough. I always thought I had to be the best at everything, better that anyone else. Perfection. The problem was that I was always comparing myself to the wrong people. I needed only compare myself to *me* because there will always be greater or lesser people. It just *is*. Perfection is also very boring, so I chose personal excellence. Once you're perfect, there's nothing to improve.

I found peace in a quote which I never forgot;

"What I do doesn't have to be perfect… it doesn't even have to be good… but it does have to be *mine*."

Belief and Trying

I read the following in a magazine, and as we all know, if it's in print, "it has to be true."
Riiight...

I apologize if I've mis-gotten the following initial set up, but bear with me, it WILL be worth it.

Years before his *Star Wars* epic was even a thought, filmmaker George Lucas was tediously editing his film *American Graffiti* with some of his crew one night. As it neared quitting time, he put away "Reel 2—Dialogue 2" of the movie into the familiar "can" until he came back the next day. "Hmmm," he thought, "That would make a great name for a robot if I ever do a sci-fi flick." So he jotted it down in his idea notebook.

A short while later, like many of us kids during our youth, he had a screaming sports car he liked to drive fast. Once, while showing off its speed, he proceeded to take it over 100 miles per hour down a neighborhood street. He lost control, wrapped it around a tree and ended up in a body cast from head to toe. They didn't expect him to live. Several times during his recovery he had caught himself giving up the will to live. Yet something inside him said, "No!" His inner spirit, his higher self or what he ultimately described as "The Force" brought him back.

It's my belief that this unlimited "Force" is at the core of each and every one of us. When we tap into this "Force", we are each totally capable, totally loving, and totally healthy and prosperous. But for many of us, belief in ourselves or the true picture of ourselves we see differs greatly from what we would like to be. So we *try* a thing. Long before

Star Wars I found that I can't really *try* anything.

Someone would say, "I *tried* calling you." Well, either they picked up the phone, called me and got a busy signal, got no answer, or they didn't call at all, which is usually the case. In the first two cases the call was made but the cycle was incomplete due to my unavailability. *Try* to pick a pencil up off the table. Go ahead... *try!*

You can't.

You can either pick it up or let it lie. There is no in between—or *trying*.

We either make an effort toward something or we procrastinate out of fear of the unknown, the *"what ifs"*, I call them. "Oh I'll try this thing but if it doesn't work out, I can say that I knew it wouldn't work out anyway." We become walking information booths of daily trivial statistics... heart disease, arthritis and the like. We may even read the paper on how bad the world and local economies are. We want justification on how *bad* things are so in case we're ever "poor"—be it financially, emotionally, physically or spiritually—we can pull out any news article at random as to why it happened to us. In other words, we spend our whole life *preparing to fail!*

WOW!

This brings me back to the *Star Wars* trilogy, specifically the second one called *The Empire Strikes Back*. The dialogue is between Luke Skywalker (the hero) and Yoda (The Jedi Master teacher). Yoda is going to teach Luke, through rigorous training, how to become a soldier and practitioner of the "Force". Upon completion he is to become a fully-fledged "Jedi Knight". Since Yoda was the teacher of *all* Jedis for 700 years, it's not a surprise that Luke searched the entire galaxy to find Yoda. Luke finally located him on a slimy jungle planet. Upon attempting to land, he crashes his space fighter, cockpit-high, into this yucky swamp. During one of their training sessions, Yoda encourages Luke to use the "Force" he is learning about, harnessing it to help him levitate his spaceship out of the swampy water and onto dry land. Luke replies that it's too big an object. Yoda implies that he knows it's possible and so the conversation goes:

LUKE: OK, I'll try.
YODA: Try NOT!… Do… Or do not… There is no "try".

As Luke reaches out and begins to spiritually lift his ship halfway out of the muck, Yoda's eyes grow wild with excitement that Luke may just pull it off! But alas, Luke gives up and the spacecraft drops in even deeper than when he started. After much huffing and puffing, Luke goes back over to Yoda and says, "I can't. It's just too big."

After some angry words from Yoda, the teacher then raises his arm, closes his eyes and, harnessing the all-powerful "Force", gently raises the ship and sets it gingerly on dry land.

Luke in, utter amazement, swiftly comes up to Yoda and says:

LUKE: I don't believe it!
YODA: That … is why you failed.

'Nuff said.

Get Serious, Will Ya?

"Stop clowning around!"—"Grow up!"—"Don't be silly!"

These are expressions we have all heard from time to time. But whether it's time to be ultra-conservative "stuffed shirt" corporate serious, or "full-tilt" Bozo-the-Clown crazy in your daily dealings with people is a judgment call.

'Tis a fine line we tread and which way to act appropriately usually depends on who you're talking to. Yes, there is a time to be serious and get down to business.

Yet I submit that the social pendulum has been stuck on "serious" for decades too long. Thankfully, we as a society are slowly coming around to realizing that we no longer need to be fearful of being laughed at. Most often I find that people are laughing with us.

Why?

Because mostly everyone has been in our shoes at one time or another. They can relate to the way comic relief works.

Now, when I speak of silliness, I'm not talking about having fun at someone else's expense. I am talking about putting some fizz back into the soda of life when it seems flat and giving the meter a shake when it seems stuck on "serious". This is the type of fun that you, as an individual, are capable of imparting to overly serious situations, in an effort to help you and those around you to LIGHTEN UP!

Think of it!

As an example, assume for a moment you're a real estate sales person. Those out-of-town buyers you've been in touch with for over a year-and-a-half are finally making the move to your city. You've babied them and given them the grand tour of the area. You've bought them lunches, dinners, gift cards, aspirin, and pads for their feet!

After showing them twenty-eight homes a day for three solid days, negotiating a contract for five more days, talking with every one of their financial experts to make sure they all feel it's a really great deal and getting everyone's attorney to agree, you've just finalized the signatures on a sale for them!

Phew!

You've been serious long enough.

Suddenly, the five-year-old inside you flips the "silly switch" on, you tell your buyers that it's time to celebrate, and you proceed to produce a box of goodies—everything from Groucho Marx masks and squirting flowers to Beanie Copters and balloons. You give one to each of the people with you, then instruct them to jump into the car because you're all going down to *Chuck E. Cheese*'s for lunch and a dive into the "ball crawl"!

If that idea is too wild (or too tame) for you, be creative. Come up with one that works for you…

…and send me your ideas!

It's fascinating to me how even humor has become a serious business. However, humor hasn't only attracted those with business acumen, but more recently, hospitals and health organizations as well. Studies conducted have found that laughter, especially hearty laughter, causes the brain to release endorphins. Endorphins, as many are already aware, are natural painkillers produced by the human brain. They can be up to 100 times more powerful than morphine. Hospitals are setting up laughter rooms for recovering patients. TVs, DVDs and VCRs play nothing but comedy and cartoons all day long. *The Three Stooges* and the *Marx Brothers* are the attending physicians—and guess what?

People are recovering and leaving these hospitals much more quickly, thereby saving millions of dollars nationwide in extended hospital stays. In addition, the laughter and good humor are contagious. This tends to spread to the doctors and nurses and the rest of the patients on the floor creating an atmosphere of positive and upbeat energy. In short, everyone's happier and healthier.

Just look at the explosions of comedians and comedy clubs across the country—and the droves of people they attract. Why do we naturally want to escape from someone who stops to tell us about all the bad things that are happening to them, yet a whole group of people will lend an ear to someone who says, "Hey, I've got a joke for you!"

We all know why. We love to laugh! We just don't know that it's always Okay.

Next time you catch yourself in a serious mood or environment, feel free to think of something funny and laugh out loud. Frequently, you'll find that this is enough to cause many people to laugh right along with you.

And if they don't, just smile as you walk away and say, "Hey, if I don't see you in the future, I'll see you in the pasture!"

Go Ahead… Jump!

It was August 20, 1990 when I got the news. My marriage was rocked to the core. It was the beginning, the first day of my forced acceptance of the fact that my life as a husband was beginning to end.

And now, three days later I was poised to jump. A little voice inside my head kept trying to convince me to go ahead and… jump.

I mean, after all that's what I came up here for, isn't it?

I was numb with emotional pain from the news three days ago.

Was I truly making a rational decision by jumping?

Who knows?

Yet, having planned it, I knew I had to go through with it.

It all started with Bill, an excited friend of mine I saw at a social gathering. He was a veteran skydiver and also an instructor.

He talked me into it. I told him I wanted to do it. He said, "Sure, that's what they all say." His challenge caused me to re-iterate to him that when I say I will do something, I follow through.

So there I drove… for an hour alone that August 23 morning.

I showed up at the Batavia airport on that bright sunny day to partake of the mega-adrenaline rush that the area enthusiasts call *skydiving*!

Not parachuting mind you, but *skydiving*! Parachuting was for wimps, I came to learn, just as I was to learn so many more things that day. Parachuting I had done years earlier and it was done from 2800 feet. My chute was attached to the little airplane we were all sitting in.

The "plane" looked more like a reject from an MGM back lot disaster film. It was held together with spit and chewing gum. When we all climbed in and it rattled its way down the dirt runway parallel to the cow pasture I actually felt sorry for the pilot and was elated that I, at that point, was the one with the chute on. When we got up to 2800 feet our instructor popped open the gull-wing door as the pilot slowed the plane to 70 mph Hearing the rush of the wind explode in the cabin had me check the dryness of my trousers. My chute had a little strip of Velcro protruding from the top called a static line.

This was attached to another piece of Velcro that was bolted to the floor of the plane. As I waited for the jumpmaster to scream "JUMP", my heart pounded as my one foot was on the plane and the other dangled almost 3,000 feet above the earth. As I let go of that little rattletrap my chute was automatically pulled out for me as I fell. It was a tremendous rush.

But today I was moving from 2,800 feet to 15,000! That's about 3 miles! Couple that with the fact that my chute would not be opening for almost a full minute.

Sounds short, huh?

I thought so too.

But now stop and count to yourself, "one-one thousand, two-one thousand, three-one thousand" and so on all the way up to "sixty-one thousand".

Then further realize that all that time you'd be falling toward the earth at 120 miles per hour!

That's like sitting on the hood of your car while going over a cliff and into a canyon three miles deep at 120 mph… for sixty (count 'em) seconds.

The reason for today's jump at this location was that due to a larger than usual cargo plane being on site, which is a rarity and luxury at the same time, all the upstate skydiving enthusiasts were here together. This was a plane with no obstacles or seats in it thus allowing a bunch of these crazies to jump out at the same time. Being able to jump out twenty people at a time they could do all those star-like, hand holding formations you see on TV. They even had three or four jumpers with video cameras built into their helmets with them to film the formations that they would immediately view afterward on the ground. For an extra $ 30 you can bet that I hired one of those guys to film *me* because I didn't know if this was going to happen again. I also wanted to make sure my friends believed me when I told them about it.

As I got acquainted with an instructor he told me we'd be doing what's called a "tandem" jump. That means that the instructor is buckled to my back. I found that New York State laws required me to make about forty or fifty static line jumps before they'd allow me to freefall on my own.

Back then, at about $ 60-$ 70 bucks a jump, I decided on this shortcut to one of life's ultimate rushes.

You see the theory was that even if I passed out and didn't pull the ripcord to our two-man extra large chute, the instructor, having a personal interest in his own survival, would be my "guardian angel of ripcords" and make sure we didn't hit the ground hard enough to form a crater.

As we suited up, harnessed ourselves together, and were shoehorned into this ultra-light, tuna-fish-can-of-a-plane, at takeoff I was told of the "skydiver's unspoken rule".

That is that once you have all your equipment strapped on and ready, you never land with the plane.

"Oh my God!" I thought. "That means that everybody jumps once they're in the air!" I asked how that could be. There had to be some other first-time jumper like me at sometime that got to the door of the plane at 15,000 ' that looked down and freaked out, right? They said that some people do but that they just gently pry their fingers from the fuselage and calm them down, tell them to slowly waddle back into the plane and sit down, then as soon as they turn to walk forward back into the plane, the instructor who's still strapped to their back pulls them backward... falling out the door and into the atmosphere.

"Don't people get a little bit ticked off?" I asked.

"Not really. Once they're all suited up and standing at the door we already know that since they've come this far, they'd be more angry that they didn't jump."

I knew right away that these people were a different breed.

One lady jumper was even three months pregnant and bragged to me that her baby had already had three jumps since inception.

Great.

Standing in that plane's arched doorway looking down at the farm-field-quilted earth, I'm sure I've been as scared but I don't remember when.

I thought more than twice about turning around but then remembering that I'd get yanked out the door anyway.

And then it hit me...

...I realized that this was the physical manifestation of a metaphor for what was happening with me, and my life, right now.

Here I was at the edge of a huge... no, mammoth void.

I could turn around and stay in the mundane safeness of the plane and go back to the way things were. We would all land and all would be well with the world and my life... but nothing would change. Even worse, nothing would be learned.

Or...

I could just trust that by stepping into the void would cause me to learn things about myself, my life and the universe that I would never experience otherwise. My fear of the unknown many times caused me to remain with the status quo.

But today I thirsted for more.

All my past learned experience came together and made me realize that...

...nothing is forever...

...that the only thing constant in life is change.

"Jump!" the voice of God inside my head said.

So I trusted... I let go... and I stepped into the unknown void.

The instructor on my back became my higher self or my Godspirit that was watching over me.

The step into the void was a gargantuan step of learning to trust further than I ever trusted before...

...and for the next five eternal seconds my entire being went into sensory overload.

I couldn't tell if I was falling...

Or walking... Or flailing...

Or flying.

Time and history stood still at my feet.

The torrent of rushing wind blew into my face and up my nostrils and then into the back of my throat with such force that I thought at first I'd asphyxiate, but then, change once more... My body adjusted its breathing.

By the time I came back to sensing what was happening I was fearful and ecstatic as I looked at the cameraman falling face-to-face across from me.

I cheered and whooped but was barely heard.

I looked below and slowly saw the tapestry of farm fields growing larger and larger and more colorful.

My higher power then gently tapped my side three times, the signal to pull the ripcord to open the chute.

As I clumsily yanked it out of its holder, the magnificent canvas of life-saving color inflated above our heads. It slowed our journey to the earth as the second phase of the jump turned into an amazed and awed wonderment of awareness.

Looking down, my problems seemed so miniscule.

I was even more elated that I was able to trust *something* again and everything turned out so right.

As we gingerly touched down, I was a different, more peaceful soul with a knowingness that change, especially rapid and immense change, was God's way of saying;

I believe you're ready to grow to the next level of your life. You have learned all the lessons of this period and it is now time for you to change into betterment. You are now ready to learn the next lesson…

Hand Holding Lessons

There we were at the mall. Just the three of us. Just the guys. Daddy and two sons. A four-year-old, an eight-year-old, and me... just hangin' out. We window-shopped, rode escalators and elevators, and threw coins into the "dancing waters". And the laughing and running around and horseplay was so obnoxious that, if my parents were around, they would've immediately lassoed me and lashed me to their side until they were done shopping. Maybe it was my own little way of rebelling to let my children just play and wrestle and verbally joust at the top of their lungs with each other. Maybe I loved letting them be "just kids" with all their mischievousness hanging out. Maybe... and just maybe I was having fun right along with them! What a concept... having fun as an adult!

Well, even though I know I'm going to live until I'm at least a hundred-and-fifty-years-old, I know I'll always be fifteen at heart. It's funny, whenever I tell people that, they kind of politely laugh and say, "Oh yes Rein, I thought that way too when I was your age, but now I think more realistically." I feel badly for them. It seems they now live in resignation that the spark for life no longer applies to them. The child-like, open-eyed wonderment of the newness and surprises of everyday life are no longer fun. They live in quiet desperation each day, just trying to get by, no longer having any dreams or hopes or joys. They focus on the short-range day-to-day unpleasantries of running a life as best they can. Then that focus *becomes* their life... of just getting by, and *that* being okay.

Well as for me ... I don't think so.

I submit as proof of longer life to take a look at the statistical side of health. Over one hundred years ago the average life span for a male was thirty-seven years. Women got a little older, but not by much. Yes, it was a harder existence of plowing fields with a horse-drawn plow, tending the farm animals and getting little rest plus all the diseases we had not yet a cure for. Yet that focus... that attitude of survival was typically all that people thought about. There wasn't time to have an affair or divorce. People married and had twelve kids, to have help around the farm when the parents got older, and then the natural evolution of *love* would take its course. And most of the time those early families were pretty well isolated from the rest of the world.

We all know about that scenario in today's society. Yet look at the change in today's life expectancy. The average age for a male today is high-70s and climbing daily. That's almost doubled in a mere 100 years! Plus, now the research shows that because of computers, we now learn and gather information at blistering speeds. Take, for example, that since recorded history began or the birth of Christ, all the knowledge of humankind that we've gathered about everything—we've taken 2,000 years to learn things to date. We will now gain the same amount of knowledge, about 2,000 years worth, in the next six years because of computers. So if we've doubled our life expectancy in the last 100 years and are learning about medicine and ultimately our spirit (as I feel that's where disease is created anyway), why couldn't it then be realistic to think that we could again double our life expectancy in five or ten years? Why couldn't it be that way with all the major changes globally such as the Berlin wall coming down, Russia's Communist grip coming apart, and a re-focus of political control given back to the people of each country, that our world's consciousness as a community is changing our beliefs? What if we feel we *deserve* more, that we *deserve* longer life, and thereby being able to contribute more back to society.

Not too long ago someone organized a US hand holding session.

There was a nationwide, coast-to-coast line of people holding hands from one end of our country to the other.

Now, why would someone think of that?

Why were so many people moved to participate? Even the president and his wife were there. You'd think they had better things to do than hold hands with… hmm… the rest of the country. Or was this the most important event of humankind yet? It certainly was a powerful message and beheld an energy all its own.

Just think if we all formed a complete circle around the world by holding hands with each other!

What would that feel like?

What would that mean?

I know one thing:

During that time, no one participating could launch a missile, pump drugs into their body, say a discouraging word about another, etc…

In other words, the *focus* during that moment would not have an ounce of despair or negativity in it. It would be like attempting to be sad or angry and putting a silly smile on your face at the same time. It can't be done because *both* are an attitude and you can only wear an attitude one at a time.

Well, there in the mall we sat having a snack of cinnamon rolls and milk. The boys had been teasing each other and fighting and pulling each other's shirts and throwing stuff at each other. In general, a negative focus, brother to brother. The littler one asked to go to the bathroom, and even though I knew where the bathroom was, it was still kind of far from where we were sitting. I wasn't finished yet with my snack to go with him but knew that even though I could see him and watch him most of the way, it might be tricky to go by himself.

"I'll take him Dad!" my oldest boy excitedly volunteered. I trusted he would and said, "Okay but come right back."

"We will!" they said and off they went.

And these two boys, these two children who, moments before had been negatively focused on each other, must've realized they were now briefly on their own without Dad to protect them.

About ten steps away, with their backs to me, I saw the oldest reach out his hand as the younger instinctively and then gently reached up and, yes, took his brother's hand. There they were, holding hands, holding hands—in love for each other—mutual guidance, and trust and comfort, knowing that each was there for the other.

Yes, I cried. No, I couldn't stop for about a minute. (That's a long cry for a public place you know, especially for a man! They're liable to take away my "macho" certificate for something like that!)

It's amazing that I would be blessed with these two magnificent teachers at how simple life is and how hard I make it sometimes.

Oh, by the way, I hold hands whenever I can.

Care to hold anyone's hand lately?

I know; you probably do so all the time, right?

Hope

Hope doesn't sell.
Neither does Faith.
Neither does good news.
Or so it would seem.

Yet hope is mysterious. So is faith. Even though they have different meanings in the dictionary, they are synonymous in their power. Here's one such example:

My 14-year-old son brought over his rocket for his weekend visit with me. After all, it was a perfect June day for rocketry! After finding a huge, open school soccer field away from the trees, I took stock of the speed and direction of the wind. I asked my son how far his rocket had gone at his last launch back home at him Mom's. I asked specifically how high and how far it drifts. He said, "Not that far." Having had some experience with Murphy's Law, I decided to compensate even further since he said this was a new, more powerful engine. Yup, you guessed it. A magnificent launch! Then a bursting open of the *Death Star* nosecone, four orange streamers majestically dropping to earth and behind it, on a second parachuted section, the cardboard tube body. Both heading for the trees. Miraculously, the heavier *Death Star* portion came through the myriad branches and hit the ground. But the tube section disappeared. Our four-man search party—me and my three sons—and the thousands of mosquitoes, combed the woods next to the marsh to no avail… and now we were losing light. We had to stop the search for the night. My oldest son didn't want to give up.

"I just want to know where it is," he said, choking back tears. "I spent hours putting it together and all my savings for the month to buy it. What are we gonna do?"

There's something unexplainably heart wrenching seeing someone you love in pain, to where every once in a while, the right words come out of my mouth.

"We'll come back in the morning when we have fresh light. All we can do right now is hope. Sometimes hope is all we have."

And for now, it was enough. He reluctantly agreed.

The following morning, he and I came back alone. Fully scarred by bug bites from the night before, we could now at least see! He insisted we look around the area where the other piece had landed. I stepped into the marsh, got a "soaker", fought through the brush and got scratched, stabbed, and whipped by all the branches, twigs and cattails scolding me for invading their world. Nothing. He was determined. I finally decided, through my limited physics reasoning, that the bright orange and white parachute must still be in the treetops. I scanned. And I kept hoping. I never really stopped hoping but was cautiously skeptical, had to be, to get him ready for a possible let down. The trees were over 30 feet tall. I squinted and scanned further. Suddenly, the sunlight dusted the treetops and there it was!

"I found it!" I said.

He came running. "Where?"

About sixty feet up. Against a branchless tree trunk flopped my son's rocket and chute.

"OK, now how do we get it down?" he asked.

After exploring all logical options, I said the only thing we could hope for was to come back tomorrow and see if the wind would shake it out of the trees, but it looked pretty tangled from being whipped around all night. I must admit, having lost a few kites to trees in my life, I think I lost hope. Fortunately, I kept my opinions to myself as we walked back home.

"Can we come back tomorrow and see if it came down, Dad?"

"Sure," I said.

I pondered.

Why hope when things seem hopeless? Why have faith in things and in people when so much of our world is filled with misery and injustice? The news is flooded with such stories daily. Christopher Reeve's quadriplegic state after a freak accident, missing children, war-torn countries, mudslides, earthquakes, floods, forest fires and hopeless situations I can't even imagine.

Or so it would seem.

No, they don't always end happily. Yet, I'm positive it would be an eye-opener for us all if there were statistics that showed how many happy endings were created by hope. Just look at how many of our military were re-energized to go on to the next day because of an entertainer named Bob *Hope*. Coincidence? Maybe. But if you add the seemingly endless "bad news" stories day to day, and divide by five billion people on the planet earth, what percentage of the populace was really affected? It's miniscule. Less than $1/10000000^{th}$ of a percent! And the hopeless cases that *did* have a happy ending, we'll rarely hear about. They're not interesting enough to make the news. Yet, to the little boy whose rocket got caught in the tree, hope was everything. Go ahead… hope for the best. Put out a little faith in yourself, your situations, your fellow people.

What do you have to lose?

My son's mom called me after picking the boys up at the end of the weekend. It seems on their way home, my rocket-launching, fourteen-year-old son asked his Mom to go by the woods for one last chance at the rocket. As he walked up to the edge of the woods, there it was, waiting for him on the ground, left by *hope*.

It's Really Me!

It was just another Pennsylvania-Dutch-type craft show—hut after hut of fine handiworks. They were like little houses, end to end in long, neat rows along the street, and each end had a screen door that led to the screen door of the next one. This was apparently done to separate the vendor's individual's personalities.

I was carrying one of my clothing purchases on a hanger from one hut to another, browsing. As I exited one shop's screen door to open the next, I looked in to see the back of the saleslady I was about to meet. My feet froze, stunned in my footprints as I looked at her. It couldn't be! Her back was to me but there she was! She was about 4' 10" with a plain farmer's-wife-type blouse, skirt, apron, and perpetual kerchief. She always mis-pronounced "kerchief" because when we came to America from Germany, President Khrushchev was in power in Russia. She heard his name, and thinking her headwear was named after him, the term stuck. She always called it her "Khrushchev".

My heart fluttered, a lump formed in my throat, and I began to perspire. I had missed her so much since she had died seven years ago. There was so much I wanted to say to her before her debilitating Alzheimer's disease overtook her mind. There were so many regrets of not calling her more frequently, not spending more time with her after Dad died. I got involved with my own life and affairs and lost touch with the fact that she gave me life.

Confusion ricocheted through my brain. Why here? Why now? I couldn't help the urge of wanting to burst through the door and consume her tiny frame with a bear hug.

And then she slowly turned. It wasn't her. She was very close in looks, but it wasn't my Mamma. Not a word was spoken, just looks exchanged. My face initially showing gleeful anticipation, then regret, then disappointment that was sensed by her immediately. Her life's experiences recognized my emotions instantly, and she wanted to comfort me with her eyes.

I politely smiled as my eyes saddened. I lowered my head and walked away. I didn't even go into her store. As I ambled out into the open lawn area toward the woods, I pondered again missing my Mamma. I headed for the nearest tree to sit down under and cry. At this moment, I missed her so.

As I turned to sit, there she was again. She had followed me from her store. As our eyes met she said, "It's really me!"

"What?" I said.

"It's really me!" she repeated.

"Who?" I asked softly.

"Whoever it is you're missing right now," she answered.

"My Mamma," I answered back.

"That's me," she said.

"But you're not her," I softly protested.

"I am for now, God sent me here for you, just for the moment… to comfort you."

I can't explain why I collapsed and dissolved into her arms, sobbing, but she held me as I cried and cried and cried.

All my sorrow and regrets spewed out to her in a torrent of emotion… to my Mamma.

She listened and comforted me for over an hour, never once thinking about her store.

I was, for that hour, once again in my mother's presence, and more importantly, in my mother's arms.

As I finished, she gently wiped my tears with the ever-present Kleenex she carried in every pocket and sleeve, kissed me on the forehead and said, "I love you and I'm very proud of you. I'm fine. Now go back and continue your wonderful life."

With one last motherly hug and kiss, she turned and walked back to her store, the work which she loved.

And that tiny frame with the "Khrushchev" was once again anchored in my heart.

That's when I awoke… sobbing.

We just never know, do we?

Meandering Thoughts of my Snowboarders

I look out of the back bedroom window and see my two boys, Nick and Phil, snowboarding on a Sunday morning. It is a crisp, cold January winter morning, the kind where the snow crunches under your boots. The sky is bright blue, the sun a fresh morning face illuminating the whole world around us.

They've been snowboarding for about an hour. They can't seem to get enough of it… sliding, jumping, falling, laughing, mocking each other and eventually landing at the bottom of the hill with an impact that scatters their gear all over the yard. In snowboarder language, that's called a "yard sale".

I looked out to make sure they were all right as I saw no immediate movement. As I observed them lying on the ground, I realized that they stayed lying where they fell… to talk.

Just talk! Two brothers, who were earlier teasing each other and trying to show to their friends that they maybe didn't care for each other as brothers, now were re-bonding.

Because they knew better.

They knew they loved each other. They knew they loved to play together.

And in the crunchy, pure white snow of a bright, cold, crisp, wintry Sunday morning, lying in a comfortable "yard sale" position, two young boys—my children—again taught me something of life.

That lesson is; when the world isn't watching, we really can let our guard down and re-love each other the way we were meant to, the way we know how much we care for each other.

Much like the people in the world.

Amen.

Meaning of Life
(What a Question!)

Ah… the ageless and eternal question is asked again:

WHAT IS THE MEANING OF LIFE?

It's amazing how many other questions that one spawns, like:

For whom?

From whom?

To whom?

And at what point in the person's life who's being asked?

I've read many a response from famous people to people globally unknown. I've asked my "significant other" at various times in my life and gotten deep, rich answers as well as embarrassed, glib little fluff-off responses.

I've read…

…and thought…

…and written…

…and thought some more.

I've searched for an answer for *me*, just in case someday a journalist, who shoves a microphone in my face for a response, would not catch me off guard. I would reply with some deep, rich, well-rounded, balanced and thought-provoking answer…

…an answer that would make the listener or viewer go, "Hmmmmmmmmmm…"

It's a great question. The type of question you'd ask at a cocktail party with no alcohol.

And you'd always get a different tapestry of remarks.

It would be like asking a hundred people a question like:

"What's the best car in the world?"

"What's the best drink in the world?"

Or give these a shot:

"Who's the handsomest man in the world?"

"Who's the sexiest woman in the world?"

Then, to really make it interesting, you'd go back to each question and ask:

"Why?"

I recall a clip of the *Tony Orlando and Dawn* show, or at least this is how I remember it:

During the last segment of Tony's show he used to turn the camera towards the audience and let the people participate in his antics. One week he'd ride the camera boom and photograph different people in the audience. The next week he'd run around quickly with a wired mike to interview people...

...kind of an early pioneer of the audience talk-show format.

Well, one particular week, as he was looking for someone to chat with, he caught a glimpse of a lady across the room. She was probably in her 50s or 60s, yet she was bouncing around her seat like a young schoolgirl type... you know, a groupie of Tony's. You could tell she was a big fan of his.

(The word "fan", by the way, comes from the word "fanatic". Don't you just love all these worthless little bits of trivia I come up with?)

As he went toward her she just about jumped out of her skin! Tony came running over and asked her to stand, BOING! Out of her seat she bounded! EEEEEEEEEEEEEEEEEE! she squealed.

The audience ate it up and roared at her exuberance. One could also tell that her "less than exuberant" and much embarrassed husband was sitting next to her and trying to crawl under his seat.

Tony put his arm gently around her waist and smiled then asked all the usual questions; "Name? Where from? Are you having a good time? Do you like the show?"

EEEEEEEEEEEEEE! She shrieked again while clapping her hands.

The best scene was yet to manifest itself when he gently leaned toward her ear with the mike to intimate a whisper but also so that the entire audience could still hear.

He asked in a soft tone; "Is this your husband?"

"Yes!" she said.

"Do I have a chance with you with him around?"

"No," she replied with a schoolgirl grin as she lovingly looked at her husband.

I mean, she didn't even think twice about her answer! "What gives?" thought I. Here's a handsome TV star with money, etc., one that she's gaga over asking her a "fun" question and in response she gives a wide-eyed, innocent, Edith Bunker-type serious answer... and *smiles to boot* for cryin' out loud!

Is that not true love in its finest form?

"Pardon me Ma'am, but what is the meaning of life for you and why?" I'd ask.

And I'd get an answer embraced with timeless wisdom telling me what it meant to her. She'd also tell me that the best car in the world is a '57 Chevy Nomad station wagon—gray. Why? Because it's a solid car that you can schlep stuff, dogs and/or kids around in with no fancy computer dashboards and fix the thing with a screwdriver and a pair of pliers... If it even broke down.

Why gray?

Doesn't show the dirt or road salt and shines up like a

silver teaspoon… yeah that's it!
It's not gray, it's silver!

Ask my five-year-old Nicholas the magic question of the meaning of life.

Go ahead.

He'd tell you about a "pincher bug" he caught in a jar along with all the bug's history and idiosyncrasies and then he'd ask you to take him bowling and then for a ride on the Bumper Cars at the nearest amusement park.

Yes, the meaning of life does have to have meaning. I must constantly remind myself to stop "doing". I'm a human "being". We are meant to achieve, yes, but at the same time be balanced enough to just *be*.

My meaning of life?

To be…

…and to give…

…and to love.

…and to emotionally be evolving to the next level of awareness or consciousness.

To reach out and pull someone up because it is said that if you help someone up a hill, you get nearer to the top yourself, even in a mundane situation.

After changing a stranger's tire once I was asked, "Is there anything I can do to compensate you for your help?"

"Yes," said I, "The next time you see someone you think you can help…in any way, pass the favor on to them, okay?"

Just as with a meaningful life…

Pass it on.

Musical Love

I didn't like my father, at least when I was a pre-teen. He always seemed to have an answer for everything. And it was never the answer I wanted to hear. Especially when it came to my drums. He also never told me in words that he loved me that I can recall. Then, exactly one month before my fifteenth birthday, he died of cancer.

As a classic violinist, Papa was born in Yugoslavia. He grew up on a farm, a hard life until he discovered his talent to make a violin sing. He respected other musicians except those whom he felt played an inferior instrument one needed no talent to play—or so it seemed. As many parents do, he tried to influence me into following his footsteps into becoming a violinist when I was three-and-a-half-years-old. Since he was an instructor of violin in Austria after the war, he figured he could teach me. It was probably like teaching your own kid to drive. Less patience would follow during our lessons and once in a while I'd get whacked on the head with his bow out of his frustration. I didn't like the violin. At school the kids teased me that it was a "sissy" instrument. My heart wasn't into it. I fell in love with the drums. I found that a lot of kids fell in love with the drums. Yet I was determined. After a while, my dad realized that I wasn't liking his old fiddle that much. His solution? I would learn to play the accordion. Yuck! If you think the ribbing I got for the violin was bad, the accordion was only safe in the presence of other accordions. I approached it with the same lack of enthusiasm. Dad pushed harder. I resisted harder. Years of lessons on each instrument yielded no more passion for each instrument but a small flame for music in general, but especially for the drums. In third grade I thought I had my chance. In music the question was asked, "Who wants to be in the school band?"

My hand shot up, "Oooh, me!"

"Which instrument would I like to play?"

"Drums!"

"Oh I'm sorry," they said, "We already have about fifty kids from the morning classes and we have more than enough drummers. But how about the tuba? We need one of those."

"Is that the only way to be in the band?"

"Yes."

"Oh, all right," I said halfheartedly. Yet I had the strategy of a third grader. I figured I'd play the tuba for a while then maybe slide into drums along the way. Year after year I was still on the tuba. But I was determined. At home I drove Mom crazy with my dreams of drumming. I used to ask her for her drumsticks. She gave me a couple of her café curtain rods, you know the kind, little metal tubes with the yellow plastic caps on them? I'd take those and go into the sunroom with an assortment of Mom's pots and pans when Papa wasn't around and whack away until the plastic caps broke off and the rods were bent. Even though I never had a drum lesson, I used to stand outside the music room when the drummers were having their lessons and listen to their instructors. Then I'd wait for them to come out and I'd ask them to teach me what they just learned and I'd duplicate it on the block wall in the hall. I learned the rudiments, the strokes and all the mechanics of drumming by listening to others and by playing my pots, pans and curtain rods. I would play along to LPs, to the music of all the great drummers and bands I could get my hands on. If I thought the drummer's licks were too fast, I would slow the record down to half speed so I could dissect the strokes.

By the seventh grade I was still on the tuba, accordion and violin. Mr. Thomas, the music teacher, asked the student musicians who would like to be in the school jazz band. My hand shot up again, "Oooh, me! Me!"

"Which instrument would I like to play?" asked Mr. Thomas.

"Drums!"

"Oh, I'm sorry," he said, "We already have about fifty experienced drummers from grammar school as volunteers. But we need a bass fiddle player."

Since I had played violin and tuba, would I like to learn it?

"Is that the only way to get into the jazz band?" I asked.

"Yes."

Oh well, here I go again. One more instrument.

Meanwhile, I was working on Mom. Any chance I got, I would ask her to take me to the music stores and look at the drum sets. I would excitedly show her all the latest drums and equipment and describe in detail the merits of each. She would probably have rather watched paint dry. But you know Moms. They listen with all the enthusiasm they can muster. I didn't know it until later that these excursions to the music store were getting to her... and ultimately, to Papa.

"Any monkey kan play de drooms," he'd say in his broken English.

Yet even though the words may not be there, the bond between parent and child is unbreakable.

It was Saturday December 6, 1966. The parents were going grocery shopping. I was to wait at home to help unload the groceries. They got in the car and Papa told Mamma, "Take me to see these drums your son likes." She took him to *Levis Music Store* where you always paid retail. They walked in and she led him to the lilac, sparkle finish Olympic drum set I had shown her only the week before.

They were $ 550.00. The cymbals and sticks and accessories were extra. My Dad paid cash. He had them put into the car. Then they went grocery shopping.

When they came home, my dad walked in and said to me, "Help your mother unload the groceries." I walked out to the car. As I got closer, I froze. I saw, in the back seat, those lilac sparkle drums in all their glory. This from a father who never said with words that he loved me! This from a man who rarely had surprises but when he did, they were huge! I started crying and didn't know why. I don't know if I ever touched a bag of groceries that day. I do know I set the drums up immediately in the living room.

"Let's hear you play something," Papa said. I began to play. The rudiments flowed out of my fingertips. The speed I'd developed with the pots and pans was now paying off. I did a compulsive drum solo right there and then. When I finished, the last ring of the cymbals was fading as I looked up and saw my father with mouth agape in astonishment.

"Where in the world did you learn to play like that?" he asked.

"You see all those broken curtain rods of Mamma's over there?" said I.

He got me my first gig the following week with the German dance band. Papa was in the audience. His friends came up to him during my performance of *Wipe Out*, a drum solo type rock and roll song, and asked him the same question, "Where did your son learn to play like that?"

"I don't know" was all he could say. Yet he was now beaming with pride.

There are many ways to say "I Love You" between a father and a son.

It's not always with words.

No More Teams

It gnaws at me constantly, the feeling that it's possible that the answer is so simple. We all see the daily headlines, "Employment up, Employment down". The Republicans say that it's the Democrats' fault when bad things happen to our economy. The Democrats say that things got bad whenever the Republicans were in power and now the Democrats are cleaning up the mess!

"Let's beat 'em!" says one team.

"We'll beat you back!" says the other team.

The competition begins.

"We're the best!" claims one team.

"No, *we* are!" say the others.

Airtime is then bought touting the stellar attributes of team #1. Team #2 buys billboards doing the same for their side.

The public starts to notice. Slowly the public starts to rally behind the team of their perceived choice, based on the information that both teams feed out. Both sides swell in population. A juggernaut is born and rolling out of control. It's called competition!

The "mud slinging" starts. The "finger pointing" follows. Both sides dig in their heels. The issues have been lost. It's no longer important what's right

…but *who*'s right! Egos run rampant!

The competition continues.

"My team, right or wrong!" becomes the slogan.

More money is spent on both sides to fuel the competition! The competition builds to an uprising, then to a revolt, and finally to a Civil War. Brother against brother, sister against sister, 'til death do us part.

Now let's go back in time.

I would've liked to have been around when our founding fathers wrote the Constitution.

I would've put some founding mothers in the room.

I'd have asked about the part that says, "all men are created equal" and suggested that we change it to say, "all people are created equal."

I would've asked them to invite about fifty or more of their distant neighbors who didn't have a lot of money or who didn't own a plot of land or maybe were even homeless in that society, to sit in.

In other words, eliminate the dichotomy of having only the rich and powerful of their day decide on the rules for the entire society.

I also would've demanded adamantly that no *teams* could ever be established. That would mean that we'd have no more cross-party bickering between the Democrats, Republicans, Conservatives, Liberals, Independents and on and on.

This would mean that we'd all have to work together, united on anything that came our way. We could then proudly remain our namesake… the *United* States.

Think of all the money that could be re-directed from political campaigns, to causes enhancing the social and common good!

Think of all the energy from all the fire and brimstone that could be used to heat homeless shelters, soup kitchens or even homes of the elderly on a fixed income!

Think of all that creative human energy previously wasted on a political smear campaign that could be re-focused on finding solutions for teenage pregnancy, prison overcrowding or finding a cure for Cancer or AIDS!

Think of three possibilities of your own!

Think of them!

Just THINK of them! (I know you have at least three!)

Then write them down and send them to your representatives...

Assuming you know where to find them.

Abolish the Elephant and the Jackass? you ask.

Precisely.

And ah yes, Toto, Kansas, would never be the same.

One-Man Band Moment

There is no "right" amount of time to heal from an emotional trauma,

Everyone is different.

We all have our own time frame. The key is how quickly we learn what we're supposed to learn and then get to the next level of living.

I found that the emotional trauma of divorce was worse than facing a death in the family. At least with death you have finality.

The person dies and you're done.

With divorce, the personality you knew and were familiar with, in love with, dies but the physical form of that person is still here.

It's unbelievable to our psyche, to look at that person and not have them behave in the manner we are used to. It totally screws up our internal emotional wiring.

During one especially vulnerable time after my divorce, I recall being at play. I was on a date. The show was a one-man show about a man whose wife had just left him.

The man comes home to an empty house.

No note, no explanation.

Just vanished with all her clothes and her car.

He's in denial and disbelief.

He decides to dedicate his life to finding her and goes out to the big city with her picture. Sadly and in futility he asks all passersby if they have seen her. During his quest he spends all his money and ends up being homeless. He continues to live on the street and, from his home that is now a cardboard box, shows her picture to everyone who walks past him asking, "Have you seen my wife? Have you seen her? Isn't she pretty?"

His reason was that, "I just want to talk to the woman I married, talk to the person I knew one more time before I ask her 'why?' and then said goodbye."

Right there, in the theater I began to weep. It got so bad I had to get up and leave my date for several minutes so I could finish sobbing in the back of the room.

And that was the crux of divorce for us all, wasn't it?

The point is that the person we knew and trusted had turned into someone else… someone we didn't know.

Yet we just want to talk to the person we knew, just one more time, to just say goodbye.

But it is not to be, because once the other person is emotionally gone, they're gone.

Nothing can bring that back.

That's the first lesson of letting go.

Without learning to let go, we ourselves become prisoners.

An Oxymoron of Reason

Ever wonder why we as the human race are always contradicting ourselves?

I am repeatedly disturbed by the dichotomies in our society.

We preach and pray for world peace and unity. There's even a non-denominational movement called *UNITY*. Yet we as a human race continue to divide ourselves verbally, emotionally and spiritually. There are hundreds of different religions, which to me represent a difference of opinion of how the Bible is interpreted. It's fine to have differing opinions of meanings. That's where growth comes from, from creative discussion between people of a common goal. Did it ever occur to all the religions that almost *all* of them believe in a force like God? Even our entertainment industry realizes it. They merely veil the God-thing with descriptions like "THE FORCE" in the *Star Wars* sagas.

The opposite of unity happens when a group of people believe so strongly in only one meaning of anything that they are closed to any other ideas. That's where the "HOLY WARS" come from. They are a people that are so ingrained and rigid in their beliefs of hundreds and thousands of years ago that there's no room for growth, only destruction. Think of what good might happen if these factions actually sat down and listened to each other with open minds. Think of what good might happen if both sides, upon hearing a new idea from the other said, "That's an interesting idea, tell me more about that."

Think of what we all, even at a level of our families and neighborhoods, might accomplish if we were more concerned with *what*'s right versus *who*'s right.

There are different political parties which have opinions on how to interpret our governing laws. Their arguing and bickering again comes from who's right versus what's right.

In short, there are only two problems in the world.

They are;

1 Poor communication
   And
2 Maintaining one's EGO

I'm especially bothered by the hyphenated nationality descriptions. You've heard them: African-American, German-American, Italian-American and so on. I understand the pride in our heritages. However, keeping our heritages alive through these separation descriptions of ourselves is self-defeating. And every time you moved, you could just add on the city that you've moved to. Just like people hyphenate their heritage! For instance, you could call me Joe from Rochester. Except if I'd lived in several cities in my life, I might be Joe, a Rochestarian-Bostonian-Miamian-Texan-German-American. Or people could start hyphenating their backgrounds as well. I might then be Joe, a Rochestarian-Bostonian-Miamian-Texan-German-American-Entertainer-Entrepreneur-Car-Collector-Motorcycle-Rider-Real-Estate-Professional-Parent-Husband-Father-Movie-Buff-Adventurer-Writer-and-Part   time-Pedestrian-etc... to infinitum.

Yes I understand that a little description for each of us is important.

Yet from a micro-society standpoint, in America we would not be considered hyphenated Americans but just "Americans". Yet in a perfect world, we would all just be humans.

Well, the good news is that I strongly believe that we as a human race are more quickly than ever realizing a movement toward global "UNITY". It was most recently displayed in the hit movie, *Independence Day*. The theme of the movie is unity of all the peoples of the earth against aliens looking to destroy us as a race. The speech made by the "president" in the movie inspired the earth's residents. He called for all to work together in a common cause, a cause that threatened our very existence. Those words, however theatrical and entertainingly trite, stirred us all. And even though the critics disdained it, that "UNITY" was the main reason for the movie's success.

The metaphor, though, is powerful. We, the people of the entire planet, uniting in a common cause, a cause that threatens our very existence. Such was the nuclear threat during the cold war. Such is the threat of bigotries and hatreds and prejudices, most being generations old. And most people carrying these "torches" have forgotten or don't even know the injustices' origins any longer.

I'm overjoyed at the fact that I read in the paper as of today, that people are moving toward spiritual "UNITY" as well, as demonstrated by the fact that non-denominational worship organizations now number 100,000, compared to the 20,000 "established" religions.

You see, there is hope.

In spite of the conflicts we have, as of today see yourself as a part of the whole.

As of today, throw your ego away. Then you'll be able to say with humility, "I don't care who's right, but what's right."

And as of today, don't see yourself as a hyphenated human, but as an individual human being, and an important part of the whole of humanity.

At your core you will have the rights of life, liberty and the pursuit of happiness.

You see, I was an immigrant too.

Oz of Life

Ever notice how metaphors reflect life?

One of my personal favorite metaphors is the *Wizard of Oz.*

To me, the projection of the Wizard represents the Ego.

There we all are standing behind the curtain, pushing levers, spinning wheels and bellowing out loud. Meanwhile, on a stage in front of us there's this bigger-than-life projection of what we want the world to perceive us as, or at least what we think the world wants to see us as.

And then, voice booming with intimidation we tell all the "weaklings" standing in front of us what to do, how to do it, what they should think and ultimately to *go away!*

The amount of fuel and physical energy used to stoke all the fires to maintain this false projection is immense and endless, especially as long as there is someone watching. That's why we command them to *go away!* We don't want to be "found out". Except there's usually a little "Toto" who comes along and exposes us when we're too busy projecting ourselves.

"PAY NO ATTENTION TO THE MAN BEHIND THE CURTAIN!" Say we. But of course, by then it's too late.

Having been exposed, we finally turn off all the false projections of fire and brimstone and we can now be truly our humble little selves. Finding that people like us even more, since we no longer have the false façade, we almost collapse in tears of joy and frustration... that we even spent one minute of time in that tremendous waste of energy...

trying to get people to like what we thought would be a popular personality. As the saying goes:

> "What great thing could we all accomplish… if we didn't care who got the credit?"

Political Learning Pay

I hate politics. I didn't really care about the government until the last few years. After reading and watching political workings throughout the last decade, I thought, "There must be another way."

Just like the most crazy ideas that mature and become a part of mainstream acceptance, here might be one more.

Just as we have mandated and nominally paid jury duty, (which most people place on the pleasure scale as two notches below a root canal), I propose we have mandated and paid political assistance service. I'm not talking about taking office. I'm speaking about assisting the office of, let's say, Senator or Congresswoman to your district for a week or two. Now before disdaining it like Thomas Edison's light bulb idea, just ponder the benefits to us all for a moment. Let's look at the stats. I read somewhere that the average presidential election brings out about only fifty-one percent of the registered voters. Who knows how much that percentage would change if we could register all those voters who were eligible to vote. And since government is the most costly industry in the civilized world, this voter apathy syndrome goes something like this:

1 Only half the population is voting, thereby making all decisions for all of us.

2 Since the two major parties have most of the political dollars and the independent or conservative third party is not strong enough nationwide, the big two make most of the decisions on who to nominate, which means we still only vote for who those two

parties want us to. All grass roots attempts at forming a fourth or additional party have been squashed by voter apathy.

3 Since we then vote for their choices, we are still then in pseudo-control of our country's direction.

4 Since we have limited choices which have been narrowed down by the "money" people (career politicians), by then voting we still aren't really making a difference, so the attitude becomes, "Why vote at all?" (That's where we found defense contractors charging us $900.00 for toilet seats.

5 By becoming more apathetic, we lose interests in the candidates and the issues and we end up voting for the candidate whose name we most recognize and the issue that's most popular. Both of these have usually been created by marketing professionals for politicos with huge war chests. This further undermines the democratic process of our system as we give away more and more control.

6 After a while we just don't care anymore. We vote out of guilt or obligation that we should, but we don't think it will make a difference anyway. Campaign promises have been broken so often that we assume that even though a candidate may talk a good game before elected, we find that many times that once in office, especially the newcomer, end up conforming with what the "big boys and girls on the hill" tell them to do or they won't get re-elected.

Well, enough of that political apocalyptic viewpoint. One of the bright lights on the horizon has been the world-wide-web. The Web holds the impending threat of taking non-productive politicians out of the loop and having citizens of the country and ultimately, the world, talk directly to each other on their computers.

Now here's the idea!

We receive mandated service time working for a Senator or congress person of your own district, of which we are paid in the same way we get paid for jury duty except we make the pay more attractive. This could also be in place of jury duty when people couldn't be available the first time they were asked to be a juror.

(Yes people would still grumble about doing it. But they wouldn't grumble any more than they do for jury duty and with jury duty come times when you're making decisions on an individual's life. Why would making life better for the citizens of our country be any less important?)

Now for the benefits of the mandated assisting political service idea;

1 It would force citizens to see first hand how the system works (or doesn't work)

2 It would make the representative more accountable by having their constituents watching their decisions.

3 By getting people involved it would stimulate interest in the issues, give us the chance to share our ideas. By knowing each other on a face-to-face basis, it makes the representative more familiar and accessible to the voters.

4 A good representative will welcome this idea. If they're making positive changes, their re-election will be enhanced by the renewed spark of word-of-mouth endorsements by individual citizens. (*The best type of advertising*)

5   This would cause less money to be spent on political smear campaigns and allow those monies to be used for more productive purposes.

6   The campaigns would need to use less and less mud slinging to get re-elected and maybe … just maybe, voter apathy would shrink, more young people would register to vote, voter turnout would increase from 51 % to 75 % and someday, who knows 90-99 %?

Ah but that's too idealistic, isn't it?

Sure.

And throughout this century we also knew that the aeroplane would never fly, the light bulb would never take place of the candle, the four-minute mile would never be broken, and the Berlin Wall would never come down.

I mean, how crazy can you get?

The Ridgeway Dog

I can still remember it as if it had just happened… a lesson I could apply to life.

It was a bright, clear summer day. I was driving along the slowly crescendoing rush hour traffic behind one of those Volkswagen Beetles. You know the kind… kinda looks like a pregnant roller skate.

Darting into my peripheral vision came a shining red Irish setter. One could tell he was prancing around with his high-strung air without a care in the world. One could also tell by his playful stride that he was young enough to never have first-hand encountered traffic, much less, rush-hour traffic.

As fate would have it, his gait launched him directly in front of the Volkswagen in front of me. The driver never saw the dog coming. Unfortunately, you can imagine the rest. The other driver and I slammed our brake pedals to the floor in mutual angst.

Fortunately, I didn't have to deal with the guilt the driver in front of me had, as my vehicle stopped about ten feet before encountering the dog.

The scene that followed was played out on a stage directly in front of my hood.

The dog was obviously doomed. He howled, yelped, twitched, and generally contorted with the pain his body was racked with.

People came running from all directions to help.

That's the amazing thing to me. In spite of all the bad press there is about "bad" people, most folks will come running when there's an emergency with another fellow human being or living thing. Hmmm.

As people got closer, they reached out to help the dog. Ironically one lady got right up to the animal's muzzle and without warning had her fingers almost snapped right off by the setter's teeth.

I thought, "Wow! Here's this woman trying desperately to bring solace in her own little way to this poor animal and he just lashes out at her in his pain and takes a piece out of her hand!"

He might have even made her bleed.

Well that was it, of course, wasn't it? The symbolism was staggering. The dog obviously didn't know what he was doing, being delirious with pain and all.

The event stayed with me and as I reflected in the coming weeks and months. I thought and wondered how many times in my pain recently I may have lashed out and bitten someone reaching out to give me a helping hand. Then I went back and wondered how that might multiply manifold if I covered my entire life with that thought! "Oh no!"

Well, I guess I could go back and apologize to all those poor souls that may have crossed my path that I "bit", but it may take another lifetime. So I guess I'll just be aware from here on out and not do it…

Right?

And maybe I'll pass this little vignette on as I'm doing and possibly the world's inventory of emotional bites will diminish by record numbers.

Why not?

Sales Esteem 101

It was April of 1991 and it was time to play "catch up" with reading my mail. As I sat going through a real estate trade magazine, I began to yawn from all those "how-tos" and "nuts and bolts" of the business. It gradually dawned on me that sales could be one of the most exciting and boring businesses on the planet at the same time.

A statistic I've always remembered was that if every sales person in this country—not just a bunch of them, but *every* salesperson—stopped selling for one day, that same day production in the US would cease for six months! That's right, *six months*.

The next time someone sneers at you for being in sales, toss that little stat at them and make them bow down to you. Then have them sprinkle you with rose petals and thank you for keeping them employed.

Of course, getting that many sales people to write the same day off in their appointment book and *not* work may take some doing. Especially, heaven forbid, if a customer called that day and wanted to buy something... immediately.

"I'm sorry," you'd reply. "I can't sell you anything today. This is national NO SALE day for every salesperson in the country."

"Fine," the customer would reply. Then in their temper-tantrum, manipulative voice they'd continue, "If you won't sell it to me, I'll call someone else who will!"

"Okay," says you. "But you won't find anyone selling today." Sure enough, the customer calls person after person with the same results.

What a fantasy.

Now, to make a long story longer, as I sat reading article after article, I was struck by the fact that each article was very stoic and matter-of-fact. I picked up the phone and called the assistant to the editor in Chicago of the trade magazine. I explained to her that I thought they had a wonderful medium here but that there was not one article on the emotional aspect of selling. Not one that addressed the salesperson's feelings of self-worth. I was talking about issues like why a particular group of people (salespeople) don't feel like they deserve a day off... I mean *really* take a day off. Yes, without checking in at the office for messages just once. Unplugging the phone, turning off the voicemail and just relaxing.

I asked, "Why was there nothing dealing with how many of us give our lives to our clients? Or how to be more in balance with our families, or loving ourselves enough to be good to ourselves? How about getting a massage for ourselves... without guilt, satisfying our own needs if only for one day out of the week and nurturing that child within each one of us because we richly deserve to do just that?"

Getting back to the assistant editor, though, her reply was, "We don't have a format for that."

"Make one," I said.

She replied, "Er... ummmm... I... I'll check with the editor and call you back."

Lo and behold, she did! She said they'd like to try my idea. She asked me to write fourteen pages, which they'd condense into three. All this and afterward it would go to six committees for approval.

The acceptance letter came the following January. And it suddenly dawned on me the tremendous hesitancy there seems to be among us salespeople toward nurturing ourselves. We have to realize that by doing so, we are far less likely to burn out or even worse get *bored* out, and we'll be better able to serve our clients and customers. In short, we'll be better able to take care of business in general. The resentment toward being disturbed on our day off will dissipate and the cash and smiles from all will come rolling in.

Yes, it is okay to take care of ourselves once in a while.

So, just for today you have my permission to leave your cell phone at home and go somewhere you've never gone before. Somewhere that you've always promised yourself that someday you were going to go. Maybe even down to the park or beach and skip stones or run a stick through the water in a pond. Then get yourself an ice cream cone, bite into it and close your eyes to let all those wonderful carefree childhood memories come flooding back. Then as you recall being a kid once more, throw back your head and send up a belly laugh to the heavens.

And above all, do it with a passion… just for one day.

Remember, even God took a day off.

Santa Claus

Is Santa Claus for real? …hmmm…

That has to be one of the most profound and puzzling questions of all time. I think it's right up there with, "Is there a God?"

For now though, let's look at that oversized elf of a character that rides high in every Christmas parade. He's the one whose face graces wrapping paper and poster shops once a year and who's had hundreds of thousands of children (young and old) sit on, and sometimes crush, his great lap.

Santa is somewhat of a magical spirited soul. No one really knows why he gives away everything that he and his Elves hand-make.

We're so used to having a capitalistic profit motive behind everything we do. We feel that work must be done out of the *need* for survival. Whenever we as humans get trapped in a "need cycle", we are automatically out of control with the natural "flow" of life. As children, we just know that Santa will bring us toys and gifts at Christmas. We know he'll prevail year after year in spite of our friends and parents telling us we need to behave or to be "good" or get coal. But we know better. I feel that if I would have burned down the garage with my father's prize Porsche in it two days before Christmas, Santa would still have forgiven me in time to bring me my goodies. (I don't suggest you test this theory, yet I believe it nonetheless.)

With that in mind, it would seem that as children, our belief is that we don't *need* to work to *deserve* something. Why? Because as children that hasn't been programmed in us yet. Why then, couldn't it be, that Santa refused to buy into the need to be paid for his work of love toward the children of this earth? And if he refused to buy into that belief, think about this;

Propelled by faith alone, he and his elf population would be provided for, couldn't it stand to reason that his *faith* and *belief* in what he and Mrs. Claus were doing for the children and for their own dreams and self-worth was so strong that food, shelter, and clothing were somehow drawn to them? Who knows? Maybe there's a Santa guardian angel. Maybe Santa's magic provides all. I believe that to be true from a magical spirit like Santa.

And another thing. How does he deliver all those toys in one night?

Let's see.

One Night. What does that mean? Oh, I know it's a measure of time, but whose measure of time?

And what is time? Well, according to Albert Einstein, time is a man-made invention.

And according to physicist Steven Hawking; "time, whatever that is."

What if Santa magically stops time so that he can be in all places seemingly at once on Christmas Eve? We'd never really know now, would we, because we would've been sleeping all night. You've seen those sci-fi movies where someone's been in suspended animation and they thought that one night went by and when they woke up, all their friends were twenty years older. Well maybe Santa looks so old because he's been doing this for thousands of years. Maybe he only works four weeks a year and then goes into suspended animation himself at the North Pole. (Lord knows it's cold enough!) Maybe that's why he never gets any older-looking from year to year.

I raise these questions not so much for your thoughts that maybe I'm crazy. I do so to spark your own thoughts about Santa, the *Spirit*, the *Magic*, the *Faith*, and let us all realize that there is *always* another perspective to be pondered. There is no cut and dried angle on anything. We don't know everything and probably never will.

There's one thing I do know.

Santa is real.

Sometimes he takes on the form of a man in a red suit and white beard and plays out the part so we as humans have a symbol to focus on. Sometimes he takes on the form of the *spirit* of the loving gift-giver in the heart of each and every one of us on this one day a year. Sometimes he becomes the *magic* that happens to all of us at one time or another where an event so awesomely joyous happens to us that we can't explain, yet are eternally grateful for nonetheless. Sometimes he takes on the form of a *faith* in our selves or in our abilities, or a *love* so strong in our being that nothing can shake that faith until our dream comes to fruition.

And sometimes he takes off his beard and picks up his rod and staff and comforts me as my cup runneth over. He then goes back to work on some more miracles of humankind. I'm talking about things like the people and beings and animals of our earth living in total peace... together.

And more miracles like being truly joyous daily, even if it's a little fragment of joy. And loving one another for who we are right now. Not for what we do or for what we have or what we will be, but knowing that we are all enough and we are all perfect right here and now. All of us.

All – of – us.

And sometimes "he" transforms to "she" and then to "it" and then finally back to billions of tiny fragments inside each one of us in a place that doesn't show up on X-ray machines... A place called our *souls*.

Funny...

…some people don't believe in Santa.

Some people don't believe in people having souls. At least, that's what they'll tell you. Yet they'll never admit that they don't have soul.

I guess for me that means only one thing. In one form or another, we all believe in Santa. And because of that, Santa Claus lives.

So God bless us, every one. And keep the faith, baby.

Whatever it takes.

Silversmith's Mistake

It's at times when I least expect a "miracle morsel", as I call it, that one invariably hits me between the ears. There I was on one of my lone journeys. I was on vacation proving to myself and to the world that I could "happily" be alone if I needed to be. I didn't need to have anyone with me to enjoy life and I was bound and determined to prove it to myself and the world… so there!

As I drove down to Atlanta from New York, I stopped in all the places I always said I wanted to visit "someday". On this particular day I was swinging through Virginia. Ah! Williamsburg, of course. Someplace that might be extremely boring to a significant other, were one in my life in the near future, but to me… now… let's go for it. It was an experience all in it's own. The townspeople were in character and conversed with the tourists in the native tongue of the time period. Going from shop to shop, I wandered into the silversmith's shop. As he labored meticulously at a tiny cut out design in a silver teaspoon, I realized that patience was something one needed in abundance to do this job. A coping saw blade the thickness of a human hair was all he had to cut the silver spoon into a fanciful design. There was no margin for error as the design was so tiny that one could barely see the design unless looking very closely. The ladle of the teaspoon was divided into a tiny left and tiny right half, both cut out designs being identical mirror reflections of each other.

"What if you make a mistake?" I asked.

His answer: "Who will know?"

He was right. He was the creator of the design, not

unlike that design in which we formulate our lives for ourselves. If we make plans for our lives and they go awry, unless we tell the world, who will know?

If our plans change unexpectedly, who will know?

Even more importantly, who will care?

We can change anytime if we would only give ourselves permission to make a mistake once in a while, to change direction when changing direction was appropriate.

Go ahead, change direction…

…and if you make a mistake…

…who cares?

Success=Balance

Here's another one of those articles that comes across our desk that needs a quick decision...

...do I toss it?

Is this valuable?

Can I read it later?

If I read it, will I remember it?

Can it change anything in my life for the better?

The answer is yes...

...depending upon your mood, perception, or whether you just got into a tiff with someone. You may even want to read it in a quiet time... Naaaaah! Never happen.

I'll leave it up to you, but please read it with an open mind. For the next three minutes, think "outside the box."

It was one of those self-development leadership-type seminars, the kind we've all been to. The facilitator went around the room of about fifteen people from all walks of life and professions asking the same question of each of us; "What is the definition of success?" There were all the predictable answers of lots of money, power, status, position, and even some authentic answers of control of future events. When it came to me, I said; "Success= balance."

"Simple," I thought. He kept going to others then came back to me and asked me to expound. Bad thing, asking *me* to expound. Here it is;

SUCCESS = being able to balance having lots of money as well as having lots of time.

Lots of money + Lots of time = SUCCESS

Sounds too simple. Also sounds contraire, an oxymoron.

Well, it is, with the old definitions we have.

That's why we as a society are on this seemingly endless treadmill.

We want more so we think we have to work more in order to get more in order to look more important than we really want to be... Huh?

Exactly. It's confusing because we're confused about what we want.

And without knowing what we really want and more importantly, *why*, we endlessly pursue having and doing more and more.

We become human *doings* instead of our natural state human *beings*. We pursue goals and dreams for others without really knowing why we want them for ourselves. If we could stop long enough to really think about that answer... Think about it... What would your answer be?

A mentor once observed me obsessing about my business. I was working twenty-four/seven!

He asked me, do I see myself doing this when I'm sixty-five?

I said no.

"What would I be doing then?" he continued.

I never really thought about it. That's the point. I never had the time to think about it. I was too busy doing, not being.

He continued, "When you're lying in a hospital bed with a stomach full of ulcers, your family and friends will be by your side, your customers and clients will pick up the yellow pages."

Ouch!

I got it. I began to make different priorities. I began to make time for family, children and friends. Making money was important too, but not at the expense of being out of balance with my life. At first it was extremely hard. I didn't want to let go. No one could do it as well as I. Then I took my first day off. I mean really *off*. I changed my voicemail message to say, "I'm off today. Talk to you tomorrow." I had someone else monitor the voicemail. And no, I didn't even call in once. It was torture.

I rationalized, "If I'm not going to enjoy myself because I'm too worried about what I'm missing at the office, why do it?"

And then it happened again. A small, insignificant quote in a pamphlet I happen to glance at;

No one on their deathbed ever said, "Gee, I wish I'd have spent more time at the office."

Double ouch!

So I did it again the following week. And a miraculous thing happened. My customers and clients started praising me for taking time to re-charge myself. I started experiencing life again. *I realized that even God took a day off!* My children had grown so much. I began to *be* with them again. I began to *be* in general.

And in *being*, my business got even better with less effort. And life came back into balance again.

Every once in a while, stop *doing*…

…and start *being*.

Then you will know the true meaning of success.

German Club Recording

I don't know why I am lately having such a fascination with the past. As I sit here listening to an old German Band concert from my childhood on my reel-to-reel tape recorder that Pappa bought me in the early '60s, all kinds of emotions are welling up inside me.

The very first emotions upon taking the recorder out of the closet that it's been sitting in for at least ten years, maybe more, are about to overwhelm me. As I lift the cover off of my past, I sample the scents of my youth. A smell can transport one back into time, a more carefree time when my parents had the responsibilities, the bills, the worries and fears that I now ponder as an adult. I now begin to weep, partly in joy that such a time in my life existed so vividly and I recall it so realistically, and partly in sadness that I can't now, this minute, go back to those moments I now so fondly wish to embrace. Yes I want to go back, right now to that night I have recorded on this antiquated tape machine! Yes, right now! I want to go back and be in that magical evening that exists in my heart, in my thoughts, in my very being! I want to tell all those people tonight that they are all a very important part of me. I want to hug each one as they sit at their wooden benches and tables covered with cloth tablecloths, looking up at the stage. I can still see the tables! Tablecloths of red and white checkerboard patterns, fine print checkerboard. And not one table without mirth and camaraderie amongst their heritage of German people. And of course at each table were the ever-present glasses of merriment and silliness in the form of wine, beer, and whatever other magical elixirs to help the men throw aside their toil and worries of the day and scoop up into their arms their wives for a dance or twelve. They might even commandeer another friend's wife or woman or whatever other dance partner they could find. Yes, there seemed to be a boundless trust, friendship, love, and honor amongst all the people there. It mattered not with whom you danced, so long as you danced! It mattered not with whom you stood at the bar and shared a drink and some conversation, so long as you did it, experienced it, right then.

I have, at this moment, again been drawn back in time as I hear the band director begin to speak on the tape. He is announcing the history of the German Club and the band I played the violin in as a young boy. He's trying to get the audience's attention. Several people start clinking their glasses loudly to call order. One man, I'm sure is Mr. Dydymus, lets out a window-shattering whistle, and the room is instantly silent. The Director of the band proceeds with the facts. The translation;

"The German Club this eve is celebrating its tenth anniversary. Two years after its founding, the children's band was formed. Most of these are now young men and women…"

Here's the actual dialogue by the Director, Karl Adam:

Meine Damen und Herren, Liebe Gaeste, Liebe Mitglieder; Heute sind's 10 Jahre zeits Verin der Sonau/Deutschen gegruendet wurde. Zwei Jahre nachher wurde die Jugenmusikgruppe gegruendet. Es waren 15 mietglieder, 15 Kinder die damals begonnen haben. Diese 15 sind heute schon junge Maenner und Frauen …

He went on, "…started in 1959, ninety-seven members have gone through the band, eleven of the original members are still in the band today! We'd like to recognize them right now …'

The whole evening was magical! They all were. From the smells of the kitchen cooking all those German delicacies of Knockwurst, Bratwurst, Steamers, sauerkraut, potato salad and pastries galore... the sounds... people conversing in their native tongue in an oasis of Germanism within this cocoon of a building. Inside it were all a people, Danube Germans as we called ourselves, from a region of the Danube river... separated over the years by circumstances like war and then re-gathered in joyous celebration in a foreign land called America, a land not of my parents' and their friends' tongue. Their reminiscence could no longer relive what was unchanged for hundreds of years in what was my parents' homeland. That world was destroyed by warmongers wanting to acquire more real estate for themselves. It was a time of yearning for them of their past and they celebrated with a passion so as not to forget their past, just as I now cling to this almost twenty-five-year-old tape that can instantly take me back to that night. I learned so much from those times and those people. It seems so tragic that all those immigrants will never ever be able to go back to those days of their youth, in their own home towns, growing old with the familiarity of each other, their customs, their ways, and most of all, the people they would have been had they not been uprooted. Yet, I wonder, since they all chose to be in the event this evening, who's to say they're not happier in America, with boundless opportunities in which they still have their own little piece... inside the Labor Lyceum... 580 St. Paul St... Rochester, NY?

God I miss those nights. I miss going from being a child through the pains of becoming a young man in those evenings. It's like I had a date every Friday night rehearsal, and a date with girls I though were making me feel great inside, even though they just played in the band and they didn't know they had a date with me. I loved the concert nights too!

They were always on Saturdays. My parents would always attend. We three would arrive in the same car. We'd go into the building, they'd go upstairs to the entry gate, and I'd go into the practice room to tune up and go backstage. Then the greatest part of the evening, socializing! I guess that's ultimately why people go out anyway.

The concert would be two sets with a twenty-minute break. Then the dance band would set up. The party would last and last but it was always too short.

I get all those sights and sounds when I look at this recorder that cost almost $300.00, that my father bought in spite of Mom's protests. They even had a fight about buying it. I still touch the buttons as I did when I had it alone in my bedroom as an adolescent. I loved to fast forward, rewind, listen, record, click all the buttons and totally play with it. It's mine from Pappa with love. It's me, my past nights, my youth, all in one little primitive electronic box. I love it so. I just wish one thing…

And that is that my children recall as fondly our days now I so cherish with them and their mother as I do my past days I have on tape, in photographs, but most of all in my very essence.

I love my family now and I did back then. The difference is, as an adult, I now know how much.

The Plate-Spinner

I remember watching him on the *Ed Sullivan Show*. He walked out on stage with what seemed like hundreds of plates. In front of him was an elongated table of about twenty feet in length and standing straight up on the table were scores of thin dowel-like sticks. The object of the trick was to see how many of his plates he could get to spin all at once on every stick without the plates falling and breaking. Kind of like a juggling act but with sticks and plates.

As everyone watched, he would quickly and methodically put a plate on top of each stick and start to spin it with his hand.

First one, then two, then five, then ten. With each one he put up, he'd periodically have to run back to the others to give them another "spin" to keep them from falling and shattering on the floor.

As you might imagine, the more plates he had spinning, the harder it became to spin an additional one. It wasn't long until he got to critical mass and as you might imagine, plates started crashing down around him. He had to then run back and forth to catch the falling plates one by one and take them down. If he did it without breaking any, he got thunderous applause. Yet if he broke even one, the audience gave him what I call "sympathy applause". That's the kind that says, "Hey, nice try."

It struck me later in life that this was a metaphor for living. We many times feel that if we can get a thousand plates spinning perfectly for the world, we'll get thunderous applause! I thought of each one of those plates representing something in my life. Be it a job, a relationship, a financial issue, an activity, or even getting a project in on time and on budget.

I started analyzing how many "plates" I had spinning at any given time. I looked at how many were necessary versus how many were not. I started to prioritize which "plates" wouldn't matter if they broke (like the dusting getting done) instead of ones that I cherished (like playing catch with my child or going on a date with my wife for a change).

I used to think that my life was always a series of spinning plates with no time at all for me to just relax. And I realized that I was at the mercy of all those plates at one time or another. They controlled *me*.

It wasn't long before plates started crashing down all around me. My life was crashing down around me! That's what happened when I put up too many plates spinning. It was time to get to the end of the trick and take all the plates down one by one. After the final one was taken down, and I looked around at all the ceramic shards, I realized that I could take control any time I choose.

And that time is now.

I think I'll soak in a hot bath with the door locked, lights off, soft music… and a candle.

And you? …

The Senior "T"

At first I was impatient as I scoured the horizon, craning to see beyond the parade of cars ahead of mine.

"For crying out loud," I thought, "We're only going twenty-five miles per hour!"

So all the normal thoughts of what might be blocking us entered my cranial chamber...

Fender bender? Funeral procession? Construction equipment? Or maybe even a cyclist.

As the procession dipped into a valley I saw it. A 1928 Model "T" Ford. An original. A "tin lizzie", as it was nicknamed by the populace at the time. Having owned an original Model "A" Ford for a while, the familiarity of ownership was recalled from my memory. The memories include driving a piece of history like this vehicle—a car over sixty-years-old—and realizing how it must have felt to drive down the road in the 1930s. I would think about where all the people are today who's hands put it together on the assembly line over sixty years past and what their thoughts were... but that's a whole other writing.

Interestingly, Henry Ford's Model "T" had a top speed of twenty-eight mph and the standing joke was that you could have it in any color as long as it was "black".

As the roads in America became better the demand was for faster cars hence the Model "A" had a top speed of fifty-five m.p.h.

However, this day the senior "T" had a parade of slow moving autos behind it. And almost in reverence in my mind's eye I could see the processional cars in solemn respect for its age, tuck their back bumpers between their rear wheels, bow their hood ornaments and slowly and patiently let senior "T" lead them to a place where a two lane road would allow us all to pass. They'd be in awe of the utter simplicity of a vehicle unimpressed by the computerized dashboards of today's turbo-charged heavyweights.

Could you imagine if cars were living things, what do you suppose they'd say to each other?

Hmmm...

The Three Cabbies

It was a train trip adventure for me, my wife and our five children put together in *Brady Bunch* fashion. I had to work in New York City on a Sunday so I suggested we make an adventure of it. It worked out remarkably well in spite of a few snags.

There were mini adventures throughout but the ones that stand out vividly were the three cabbies we encountered over the weekend.

Stewart was the first. There we were at the end of the day at the southern tip of Manhattan's Battery Park area. It was getting dark early on this Saturday before Thanksgiving. Very few cabs were going by as this was the business district—buzzing during workweek but dead on weekends. There I was, the paternal leader. Everyone was looking to me for answers. There are times where being a leader isn't fun. This was one of those times. Imagine—New York at dusk, walking the sidewalks with five children and wife in a deserted part of the city, and no cabs in sight. A mild panic came over me because I knew that even if we did hail a cab, the seven of us would barely fit. We finally found a cabstand after all the children were beginning to complain of all the walking. At that point I felt "walking" was the least of our problems. Running up to the first cab in line, we flung open the doors. I hastily instructed him where to take us and at how relieved we were to find him. "Everybody out!" he shouted in his accent.

"I can't take everyone, only three or four of you!" We all got out very disappointedly after I firmly explained that separating from our children would never happen. As we stood semi-helplessly on the corner in the streetlights, I summoned the courage to melt away the panic. I do this by calling on my internal "Maverick Side", which we all have. My phrase is, "How hard can this be?" and it instantly transforms me into finding solutions. It also changes my faith that a solution is imminent.

Suddenly, we heard a horn beep. What had pulled up right in front of us was a limo that should have been retired long ago. You know the kind, dents and dings all over and mild rust beginning here and there. It's the kind that you wouldn't want to be seen in on your wedding day. But tonight was a different story. The electric window went down on my side and a voice called from the driver's seat,

"Need a ride?"

Was he kidding?

"Yes!" I yelled back gleefully.

As we all piled in, the children not only had a ride, but to them it was a Limo! My wife and I were elated! After the initial cabbie/passenger chat I did what I always do by asking about the driver's background, city and personal life, if they choose to share it. Amazing thing. No one has ever turned down the opportunity to tell me all about themselves. His name was Stewart. He was fifty-seven-years-old. He'd been driving this "hack", as he called it, for many years. His background was not originally that of a cabbie.

As he slipped into a nostalgic melancholy, he laid out his life to me while my family was teasing each other in the back section. He told me he used to be a successful car dealer but had lost everything to a gambling addiction when he was in his late-forties. He had also lost his previous marriage but was now in a happy, positive relationship. What he was doing was dangerous. "Hacks", I learned, were frowned upon as taking business away from "legitimate" cabs and limos. If he got caught picking us up he could be fined or even lose his driver's license. But basically he was in the city he loved. It was his home. He had a lifestyle he was comfortable with, a family he cherished and a wistful melancholy of memories here. To him it was worth the risk. He'd lost everything once already and after you lose everything at least once in your life, nothing seems to bother you that much anymore. Part of me was envious of his calm nature. He had a special inner peace many people never know.

Steven was next. A Russian Jew only in this country for a short while. He picked me up Sunday morning to take me to my speaking engagement across town. Steven was so eager to please me that he was uncomfortably over polite. Everything was "Yes sir" and "No sir". I engaged him to tell me about his life. He was working to support his wife, three children, and his parents who also lived with him. And he was honored to have his parents in-house. He was overjoyed at his whole family being together in the US because compared to what they came from, this was heaven.

Yet I heard something different when he told me about his life.

He would drive his cab for thirty-six-hours straight most days, go home for a few hours, eat, sleep, clean up and go out for another thirty-six-hour shift. Amazingly, the thirty-six-hour shift was by choice! When I asked him why, he responded in his broken Russian accent: "For my children and for my parents. I owe my parents my life and it is the honorable thing to do. It is also for my children, so that they may have more than I had. I tell them always to go to school, get education. Otherwise their punishment will be that they end up like me, their father by driving cab thirty-six-hours at a time." He spoke from his heart. His wasn't a "have to" mentality. He wanted to do what he was doing, and he meant it. No regrets.

"For the children, for my children," were his words. Those words stayed with me.

I immediately counted my blessings. His plight hit home for me, as my parents were immigrants as well. They gave me a strong foundation of work ethics and I knew I didn't want the hard life of farming that they had lived.

I had hoped Steven wouldn't fall asleep at the wheel with me in the back. He did sit idle at a few green lights though. How impressed I was at his courage! I again felt a partial envy at his spirit.

Then there was Desmond, from Jamaica. My work was done at the end of Sunday. Desmond picked me up to take me back to my family and the train to be caught home that night. He pulled up in what just happened to be a crisp clean mini-limo. It was all the cab company had available, so I got the same regular rate. What I'm most amazed at constantly is that I and my family regularly attract exactly what we need at any given moment in time. Here again was the proof. There were seven of us with baggage that needed to go to the train station. A regular cab wouldn't have worked. But there was Desmond and his mini-limo, just as if I'd expected it. He was in a suit, very polite, and the car had just been washed and vacuumed. He felt a true pride in his work.

His story was that he had been here for several years, separated from his family. He was working at getting his wife and child their appropriate papers to be able to move to the US with him. He was going to school at night for a degree and driving during the day. He'd had a rough morning. Apparently some other cabbies were mocking him at how he looked and at how clean cut his car and personal appearance were. They were obviously jealous. I told him to keep doing what he was doing. He was what I wished all drivers would be like. He was being hard on himself because he was a normally positive person and he'd allowed these so-and-sos's to bother him. I am also very positive so after encouraging him for a while, we both sparked with positive tools and attitudes we could use to combat people and issues like that.

We made each other so happy and had such an animated talk that I didn't want to leave him. Neither did he. Upon pulling up to my hotel, I asked if he would wait for me to go up to my room, get changed, and take me and my family to the train. He said, "Absolutely, sir!" We connected. I loved him, too. He was remarkable with my family, as well.

Well Stewart, Steven and Desmond, I bless you all. May you continue to follow your dreams with success and continue your teachings of people like me. You all reminded me of much that I have taken for granted in my life. Stewart of inner peace after catastrophe, Steven of enthusiasm, spirit and courage against huge odds, and Desmond of how powerful a positive outlook can be even when separated from loved ones in a strange land.

In NYC, cabbies meet people from all over the world. They are this country's first teachers to many.

And from the mouths and hearts of cabbies, that weekend, came truths. It also brought the constant reminder to be gentle with each other and with ourselves because we all… have our own story.

A Thank-You Note To My Children

It's been said that the older I get, the more I have to learn. Never has that been more evident than as a parent.

As a child, I could never see myself as a parent. Could I imagine someone coming up to me at eight-years-old and saying, "What would you tell your children when you grow up?" That would receive one of those "looks". Yet now, as the parent of my most wonderful kids, it makes perfect sense.

When I was little, I always listened to my parents, as they were my caretakers and security. If Papa told me to do something or not, it usually got done. Yet when it came to character and moral issues, I rarely listened to them but *always* watched what they did. My father was a heavy smoker of cigarettes without a filter. He died of cancer as so many others who didn't know about the dangers. I don't think that would've stopped him anyway. It's no different today. Yet he never lectured me on the morals of smoking, probably because he knew as my parent, that I was watching him. And I respect him for not proselytizing.

I found that my children also watch *every* thing I do. It's frightening to always have to be on your best behavior, especially if you know me. I'm a bit zany all the time. I could go off on a tangent at the breakfast table trying to get a laugh out of them, but of course, they've heard all my jokes a zillion times so they cause me to be "fresh". My kids have turned out rather remarkable, in spite of some natural bumps in the road from me. Because on my way to wanting to be the best parent I can be, I made a *lot* of mistakes. I'm still making them. The benefit, of course, is that I learn so much from my mistakes. And I learn so much more from my children. And I hereby want to thank them for so many wonderful moments past and yet to come.

To my children, I want to thank you for…

…always having me be on my best behavior, because there's plenty of bad behavior in the world already.

…for letting me love you my way with hugs and kisses, even though I might have embarrassed you in front of your friends.

…for laughing at my stupid jokes just to make me feel good.

…for forcing me to behave the way I wanted you to behave.

…for reminding me every day how to be a kid.

…for lying to me, because after the truth came out, we were both again reminded about how important trust is.

…for reminding me that sometimes the best thing in the world is just snuggling on the couch under a blanket with you and watching TV.

…for letting me make mistakes and have you forgive me for being human.

…for knowing that you'll make mistakes too and that they are not a personal attack on me.

…for reminding me that I can either be your buddy *or* your parent, but not at the same time.

…knowing that it takes tough love to do the hard, loving stuff for both of our good.

…for realizing that I need to be a good parent to you first. All the other stuff will then fall into place.

…for not staying mad at me too long for grounding you because you now know I did it out of love.

…for showing me that I can say "I'm Sorry" when I'm wrong and have it be one of my strengths.

…for asking me to play catch, try your skateboard, show you how to run through the rain-flooded street in your bathing suit, watch that "pro" wrestling show on TV, or to play golf in the woods, trees, water hazards and sand traps.

…for letting me learn that I don't need to know every dumb little thing you did behind my back. I know you suffered your own consequences.

…for listening to my "lectures" on life, philosophy, and right and wrong, even though I saw you rolling your eyes every time.

…for letting me rant that there is a huge difference between a mistake and malicious intent.

…for reminding me what's important on a daily basis, love, family, health, sunsets, pollywogs, your most important issue at the moment, talking with me, love, giving everyone their dignity, helping each other, love, friendship, self-respect, self-love, taking responsibility for yourself and love.

… and most of all, for loving me back.

After I'm Gone...

The house was quiet. I was alone. I went down the stairs into the finished basement on my way into the room in the far corner of the cellar I now called "my office".

It was maybe a millisecond of thought that stopped me in my tracks. My feet were suddenly un-moveable, almost cemented to the floor. And I was forced to slowly look around.

Straight ahead I saw my workbench, parts of it extremely organized, other parts askew with unfinished projects and tools strewn. The far left boasted a huge red mechanic's toolbox on a stand, under which were spare little screws, nuts, nails, glue, and every kind of fastener known to civilization. All were in assorted coffee cans and clear little baby food jars. Pretty much your basic, everyday tinkerer's fix-it shop.

Nothing special.

I wasn't seeing things as myself though. For some reason I was looking at these items as if I were someone else. It was as if I was being forced to look at life, my life, in a whole new way, an eerily peaceful way.

It was as if I had died and I was now going through my life's possessions almost as another person who would have to sort through my "stuff" as an executor.

I began to look, to really look at who I was, based on these material possessions. I saw the tools that were my dad's. Most I kept for emotional reasons. Many were obsolete by today's standards but very functional. My showpiece though was the "Army Sized" vise that I had salvaged years ago from the new owners of our old house. I expanded my observations to nearby photo albums of the past. I began to see myself and my life with a new awareness and perspective.

What would all these things mean about me to someone who never knew me? A stranger might even see these things I thought important through the photos or types of books I kept for reference. They'd see biographies and autobiographies of people I wanted to know more of. There was no rhyme or reason to who I found fascinating. I devoured these because these people's lives gave me insights I hadn't known before. There was Sam Walton, Bill Cosby, Ann Margaret, George Burns, Lee Iacocca, Donald Trump, Michael Jackson, and one of my favorite humanitarians, Albert Einstein, whose humility was overwhelming. Einstein once said, and I paraphrase, "When you sit on a hot stove for a second, it's too long but if you talk with a pretty girl for an hour, it's too short. That's relativity."

There were photos of me performing as an entertainer and musician over the last thirty-five-years on various instruments and in various forms. There were blow-ups of some of my vehicles, like a 1930 Model "A" Ford Roadster with a rumble seat, a 1971 Dodge Demon 340 racecar and assorted motorcycles. There are scores of clippings of newspaper articles over the years plus clippings of "Positive Attitude" stuff, inspiring quotes, sayings and poetry. This person, this stranger now going through my things would get a further glimpse of my adventurer spirit. They'd find several skydiving certificates and photos of me in the parachute, hot-air ballooning pictures, a photo of me in a glider in Germany. On my walls were scores of photos in a collage style… my family, my wife and children, lots of children… making memories always, or at least for me.

There were yearbooks with inscriptions from past lovers, over seven years of receipts and cancelled checks and collectible model cars. There were photos of musical instruments, many of which I still own and can still eek out a song on. Oh but what music I make… not for its musical prowess, but for the deluge of memories that comes with each song. The first kiss, the stirrings of hormonal youth, the new smell of the first car, and the joys and tears of the exact place I sat and what I was thinking when each song ran through my heart.

Yes I know every life has a story. Each is similar in its myriad details of both animate and in-animate beings.

Yet for me I've found that it comes down to only this, and that is:

Life, during life, must be lived.
And during that life, the only thing that matters is the people in it and because of it.

After I'm gone my material possessions will be sold in a household sale for one-tenth of their original cost. Yet the people who were enriched, enraged, inspired, or moved to do or be something greater than they thought because of some little thing I did or said… *that* to me is living!

I never aspired to be a great man, but only to pass on to my children…

… a life of living.

Made in the USA
San Bernardino, CA
13 September 2013